Sahara

THE ATLANTIC TO THE NILE

To Mitsou,

wife and mother,

without whom nothing would have been the same.

A. S & B. S.

Alain Sèbe ~ Berny Sèbe

Sahara

THE ATLANTIC TO THE NILE

HACHETTE
Illustrated

Hoggar: Tezouyeg and Souinan peaks (Algeria)

The call of the desert

The desert ensnares, mentally and physically, transforming those who journey through it and enticing others who have only heard of it. Awesome to those who live at its northern and southern borders, a natural habitat to those who have made it their home, the Sahara has attracted generations of travellers unable to resist the lure of the world's largest desert. Tales of the great desert entice travellers, evocative words and images capture its extraordinary beauty. The Sahara has a unique appeal; unless born within its boundaries, those who experience it choose to do so. Destiny or heritage plays a part in the lives of desert dwellers or seekers. Thirty-five years ago, a commission from Fernand Pouillon, the chief architect in charge of several major Algerian projects, took my father, Alan Sèbe, a young photographer from Nice, to the great southern desert. When I was born twelve years later, the Sahara had already become a deep and enduring passion in my family. I took my first steps in the desert when only nine months old. For both father and son, the fascination was instantaneous. As a photographer, my father travelled more and more to the Sahara and my imagination was fired by the images that he brought back. Heedless of financial constraints, I lived for our frequent trips, magical passports to months of untrammelled freedom.

Like the sea, the Sahara provokes deep and overwhelming emotions that are often described in a language of love. The vast expanses of windblown sand evoke intensely romantic expressions: travellers describe themselves as 'impassioned', 'enamoured', 'enthralled' by these spaces. This powerful passion was felt by the early explorers, whose exploits were comparable to those of the Knights of the Round Table. One such adventurer, René Caillié (1799–1838), returned from Timbuktu, his body and spirit tested as if he had made his way into Arthur's forbidden kingdom itself. Like the sea, the desert inspires and bewitches, its magic endlessly absorbing and engulfing all the senses. The nomads who scour and scrutinize the semi-barren soil bear witness to this. They hunt for forgotten traces behind rocks, sniff the scent of the sand-laden wind from the south, listen for the merest echo of a rockfall that might indicate a moufflon and savour a single leaf of a plant whose qualities have been valued for generations.

Caressed, confused or chafed by the whistling wind of the desert, thousands of different nuances strike the ear. The constantly shifting sands vibrate underfoot, loose stones on the plateau clink crystal-clear, the moula-moula bird cheeps – add the sounds of braying camels, the creak of saddles or the whirring of a partridge's wings and you have the musical cacophony of the desert.

The sense of touch is also stimulated. Sandstone scrapes the palms while climbing peaks at the heart of the **tassili** (sandstone plateaux). Sand tickles the soles of the feet, the desert wind lashes the face and, later, a cooler evening breeze from the **reg** (gravel-strewn plain) brushes past the cheeks. In mid-winter the air is dry and cold and the sun's rays infuse bodies with warmth. The coarse outer skins of desert plants or the delicate down of tiny acacias offer their own tactile experience.

The imminent storm can be sniffed when the air of the plains is heavy with warm dust. The scent of the morning dew turns every **markouba** (dense grassy bush) into an incense burner. The subtle odour of grass may signal precious water hidden in a rocky crevice and the nostrils can capture thousands of flavours, including tea, smoked millet or meat gently cooking on the embers.

Tassili N'Ajjers: Ti-n-Merzouga (Algeria)

The sensory experience is also intensely visual. At dawn, the last phosphorescent rays of the moon linger on the stark silhouettes of the landscape. At sunrise, the fresh light of dawn sheds its pure, strong rays on the desert, turning shadows blue, saturating the sky and making reflections dance on the bright sand. When the sun is at its height, the eyes must be protected from the glare and in the late afternoon, as the intensity of the rays diminishes, mirages gently evaporate. Eventually, as the autumn of the day arrives, the light casts a russet, burnished tinge over the desert, as intense as it is fleeting. The evening sky is bright and limpid, flaming briefly as the sun meets the horizon, turning gradually to a dark blue as the light fades. Dusk heralds the arrival of the evening star, sky and earth merge into one and the horizon becomes an immense space. Finally, night falls and the constellations become visible overhead, with the Milky Way trailing its silver scar over the roof of the sky. When the moon appears the stars are overshadowed but the reg sparkles with thousands of silver reflections. The pallid light is the signal for nocturnal creatures to emerge.

A few centuries ago the Sahara was **terra incognita** and still remains a force to be reckoned with for those who fail to respect it. Despite man's attempts at control, the desert remains unpredictable. It is impossible to love it without accepting the elements of risk it poses, which can range from dying of thirst to drowning, like Isabelle Eberhardt, who perished beneath the rubble of her Ain-Sefra home, carried away by the impetuous flood of a wadi. The desert first makes itself felt in one's flesh – lips bleed in the harsh dry wind, the skin of one's thumbs cracks when lashing down the baggage and fingers are lacerated by the bark of the acacia. The soles of the feet become hard, cracked and calloused from rubbing on the leather of sandals or on the pebbles underfoot. Sandstorms choke and dry eyes turn lids to sandpaper.

All of this joy, pain and effort are behind the photographs in this book. They were not taken by chance – each one is the result of careful thought, calculation and preparation. Alain Sèbe would wait patiently for a stubbornly lingering mist to clear or for the intensity of the light to alter, in order to enhance the picture he sought to take, although sometimes he would have to reject disappointing results. He was less concerned with technical expertise (second nature to him after three years at the College of Applied Arts in Vevey, Switzerland) than with the convergence of the vital components of a successful photograph. The camera became an extension of his hand and he paid it as little attention, focusing instead upon the images or details that captured the essence of a place or on the emotion excited by a planned or accidental encounter with a site or landscape. The fundamental keys to his approach involve the structure of the photograph, its content, the balance of the composition, the play of the light and the way colours complement each other. A further element in this finely calculated combination is the ability to capture a subject in motion. Of a scene lasting many hours, one sees only a fraction of a second.

Given the length of time spent in the desert, these images taken by Alain Sèbe represent a mere hint of his Saharan experience. In his pictures, however, you can sense the ostinato of the breeze or the prestissimo of the sandstorm, grasp the scale of the immense regs that reach to the horizon or visualize the overwhelming tassilis and ancient traces of encampments and caravans. Alain spent thirty-five years collecting these images. Take some time to appreciate them.

Fezzan: El-Hassi (Libya)

The land of petrified seascapes

Morocco

Morocco lies at the junction between the Arab and Berber worlds. It marks the transition point between grass and sand and it is a region where all the transitional nuances between desert and non-desert can be detected. Along its Mediterranean and Atlantic coastlines, Morocco is a seafaring country, and its northern and eastern regions are home to the stone-strewn hammadas (plateaux) that are typical of the Sahara. The Atlantic Ocean regularly batters the crenellated fortifications of Essaouira, yet just a few hours' drive to the east, in Tafilalet, the stony ground seems to undulate in the harsh light. Inland, an ocean of minerals stretches as far as the Nile.

From their palaces in Marrakesh and Meknes the Sultans would to gaze towards the desert, from whence the slave-caravans would emerge. They sought not only to control the markets but also to achieve greater proximity and access to points of supply. Coveted by powerful overlords, the desert was feared and respected by those who lived among its oases because of the dangers of drought and lurking brigands. You won't get far if you go wandering along desert tracks where ochre-coloured reflections dance on the dust-laden sand. You will soon be brought to a standstill, however, since every aspect is expertly designed to protect desert dwellers from both the wind and the thieves from the south. Even the clouds from the Mediterranean are held back by the Atlas Mountains, which mark the transition between the humid world of the north and the dry southern landscape. Their southern flanks merge into the dust of the desert. Closed to Christians and peopled by nomads fiercely proud of their homeland, the Moroccan south focused interest on these tribes living on the margins of what was described with awe and fear, even in 1900, as the 'great desert'. Between the wars, painters and writers followed in the wake of officials, sending back idyllic images of the area, full of glorious light streaming into the maze of the casbah, finely carved palace stuccoes and mysterious figures darting into **agadirs** (fortified barns). Sketches, paintings, writings or glass-plate photographs all celebrated the pure light of Morocco, its wide, wild, exposed landscape and the whistling of the **seguias** (irrigation channels) in the gardens. Interest in nearby Sahara grew but access remained difficult and care was required when travelling in the western outskirts of the Sahara, from whence bandits might swoop from the far side of the bare hammada.

Men have always been drawn to untamed regions by the lure of the unknown. Some have felt it so strongly that they deliberately risked the peril of encounters with the enigmatic hosts of the desert. One such was Michel Vieuchange who lost his life in the 1930s trying to enter the 'forbidden city' of Rio de Oro. Captured by a powerful and xenophobic sheikh in Smara, the walled city that offered fierce resistance to French and Spanish interests, he was turned out into the desert, at the mercy of the winds and the sands. Fifty years earlier a young French officer, Charles de Foucauld, disguised himself as a poor rabbi and gained valuable knowledge of the Arab world in Morocco, whose doors were firmly closed to Europeans at the time. His book **Reconnaissance au Maroc** ('Reconnaissance in Morocco'), published in 1885, gave him the credibility he needed to pursue the Saharan projects that were ultimately to bring him fame as a priest who saw his vocation as 'to carry the Gospel to the most abandoned ... not by preaching it but by living it'. Today, access to these regions is free from such perils, but in places traces of more uncertain times are evident. A sign in Zagora, at the point where the road becomes a track, warns: 'Timbuktu, 52 days by camel'.

Anti-Atlas (opposite)
Atlantic coastline: Foum Agoutir (preceding pages)

The Anti-Atlas range marks the transition point
between the snowy peaks of the High Atlas and the arid and stony ground of the Saharan hammadas.
The exposed mountain landscape shows clearly the titanic battles undergone by the plates of the earth's crust:
the almost vertical pleats of the geological strata testify to the powerful tectonic movements
and pressures that created the Atlas mountains in the Tertiary period.

(above and opposite: in the Tazenakht region)

The Cleuch tribe of Ameln Berbers spreads over a number of villages
around Tafraoute, in an area bounded by the Anti-Atlas mountains.
Built deep inside a valley hollowed from barren granite, or even on its slopes,
the Ameln villages (see Oumesnat, opposite)
are in harmony with their natural surroundings.
Those who have chosen to remain there cultivate their gardens and palm groves with great care,
their streams and ponds representing their lifelines
(above, palm grove in Timkyet).

Harvests were protected from thieves
in fortified sun-dried brick barns known as *agadirs*,
their thick walls sparsely punctured by narrow windows and a large, heavy wooden door.
The simple but elegant structure of this *agadir*
in the Ounila valley, built near a threshing area,
is highlighted by the gentle rays of the setting sun and the prettily flowering oleander.

Few travellers make the time or effort
to see Boumalne du Dades.
Nevertheless, this village on the southern slope of the High Atlas range
hosts a large local market every Wednesday,
where traders from Marrakesh or Casablanca come to sell
their fancy goods or a selection of popular Egyptian songs.

Markets

Markets are the highlight of Saharan social life. Farmers, caravan drivers, merchants and customers gather together, selling, buying, bartering.

In days gone by, business was rather different. Figs were traded for millet and slaves from the 'Nation of the Blacks' or Bilad-Al-Sudan were among the merchandise on sale. Nowadays, automobile parts are sold alongside spices and sheep. In El-Kufrah there is even a shop specializing in spare parts for trucks making their way to Chad or the Sudan. Markets play an important social as well as commercial role and act as informal communication centres. Gossip and general information are exchanged as deals are done.

Left to right and top to bottom: markets in Koufra (Libya), Douz (Tunisia), Douz (Tunisia), Tamanrasset (Algeria), Essaouira (Morocco) and Agadez (Niger). Opposite: Ghardaïa (Algeria).

The construction of homes made from earth has a distinct advantage:
the material used comes from the very spot where the house is to be built.

The framework is made from trees that thrive in the local climate.
The people of Aït Bou Guemez in the High Atlas mountains
use poplar trunks (see above) whereas the people of Aït Ben Haddou
(see the main *ksar*, opposite)
use palm trees as beams
to support the palm roofs
of their adobe homes.

The villages of the Ameln valley (opposite, Adai)

blend into the landscape with their painted pink, brown or ochre façades.

In contrast, Smara (above) forms a huge silhouette in the middle of the reg.

Built entirely from scratch in 1896 by Sheikh Ma-el-Aïnin,

it was to become an important political and religious capital.

The undertaking was of enormous proportions:

materials were transported by sea and then on the backs of donkeys and camels.

It involved a palm grove, wells and canals, and for the first time in the Sahara,

an elegant palace was built to assert a sheikh's power.

Despite its splendour, the city fell into decay after French troops entered it

in the spring of 1912.

Water

Whether stored, conserved, in wells or canals, water is the daily preoccupation of those who live in the desert. Assuring a supply is rarely easy, wells have to be dug or canals built, and many wretched men lost their lives, crushed under the debris of a foggara (underground system of water conveyance) that they were digging or maintaining.

Every water source attracts those who live in the area and is often the scene of lively local activity, busy with people and animals. An **aguelman** (natural reservoir) depends on rain or floods and consequently often runs dry. Nomads are vigilant in checking water levels before they depart. Less at risk and a more reliable source of water, wells may nevertheless still send back a sinister, dry echo when a stone is thrown in. Disappointed travellers must then journey on, hoping to find water at the next location.

Left to right, top to bottom: Lake Mandara (Libya), Ti-n-Tarabine wadi (Algeria), Ti-m-Missao (Algeria), Aguelal (Niger), Silet (Algeria), Atakor (Algeria). Opposite: Timimoun (Algeria).

Sheep play an important role
in the health and well-being of those who live in the Sahara.
Where there are sheep, there are people.
They can be seen everywhere from the slopes of the Atlas (see opposite)
to the banks of the Nile.
The docile creatures allow themselves to be guided by the shepherds
even when the meagre tufts of grass on which they graze
are succeeded by barren, stony ground.

Under the watchful eye of Tanit
Tunisia

Several archaeological sites in Tunisia feature Punic steles, adorned with Sibylline figures, the crescent moon or a man with arms uplifted in prayer. They all evoke Tanit, goddess of fertility who, along with Baal Hammon, watched over the destiny of the Carthaginians. In the 6th century AD, the Phoenicians landing on the coastline created a Mediterranean-trading empire in what is today called Tunisia. Descendants of seafarers, they had already conquered a number of inland tribes. Several centuries later the Romans were to follow their lead by establishing colonies on the fringes of their North African territories, on the edges of the desert. Soldiers too old to fight were encouraged to settle and bring up families to consolidate these outposts of the empire.

In due course, French soldiers built forts on the edge of the desert, following in the footsteps of their Roman ancestors. We discovered one in Sabria, under a leaden June sky that robbed the dunes of any contours or relief. All that could be detected was a blurred outline, the milky grey of the sky melting into the beige of the overheated sand. It appeared suddenly: a building made of raw earth, camouflaged by nature until we were nearly upon it. Sand had invaded the interior of the small fort and the sifs (sand dunes) reached the ceiling in parts. Outside, the wind-lashed frontages were swamped by the dunes whose peaks lapped the roof where sentries once dominated the surrounding area. Currents of air whistled and died in the last remaining nooks and crannies.

The sand waves of the Great Erg threaten to engulf hastily abandoned remains but don't put a stop to local initiatives. Cultivators defend their patch of ground against the onslaught of the sand and risk danger by planting new palm groves around artesian bore holes, forming lush and intermittent green patches on the ground. Snowploughs are used to clear the roads of sand and the towns and villages are busy with markets, in which spices, sheep, teapots, automobile headlamps, kid goats and Middle Eastern audiotapes are among the varied items for sale. Fierce haggling takes place while happy purchasers lead stubborn goats away or bear hens to their destiny by the wingtips. Teapots gurgle on braziers, awaiting the closure of the markets. Travellers easily pass unnoticed through this busy scene.

Alain Sèbe was certainly struck by the intensity of life in Tunisia, reinforced by the relatively small size of the country. Distances between centres are reasonable and the roads are rarely deserted. Even in remoter parts, the chances of meeting a family of nomads are fairly high. The network of town and villages is so dense that you are never far from one or the other. The resulting variety makes it easy to see the great diversity of Saharan life, including the encampments of the Great Erg, the oases hidden in the gorges, the lush palm groves or the ancient dry-stone buildings. However, the mirages of Chott-el-Djerid remind us that these towns owe their existence and survival to a very precarious balance of nature. The goddess Tanit should keep a close eye on them to ensure that the call of the oases can still be felt by generations to come.

Opposite: Ksar Ghilane
Previous page: On the edge of the Great Eastern Erg: Mahbes wadi

Nestling between Chott-el-Djerid to the south and Chott-el-Gharsa to the north,
a small cluster of dunes marks the most westerly point of the Great Erg.

In the distance, the sand gives way to a monotonous plain, dotted with clumps of ragged vegetation.

You have to head further north before the steppe becomes green.

Not that long ago, Ksar Ghilane
was little more than a thermal spring around
which a few oasis-dwellers eked out a difficult existence.
The peace and tranquillity of earlier days has now been disrupted
by its transformation into a tourist centre.
The oasis has lost some of its character,
despite the silhouette of an ancient fort that watches over the dunes (opposite).
The disadvantages of progress must be measured against the piped water enjoyed by
the goats, sheep and camels gathered above.

Of all the vegetation to be found in the Sahara, the date palm is by far the most useful and versatile.
Its fruits nourish both humans and animals, the trunk is used in construction,
the wood fibres make ropes and the leaves baskets.
Unsurprisingly, palm trees are ubiquitous and an oasis is judged by the size of its palm grove.
The oasis of Tamerza (above) flourishes at the foot of a waterfall while in Chebika (opposite)
the trees keep a foothold among fallen rocks in the depths of a gorge,
drawing their moisture from a tiny stream of water that struggles through the clayey earth.

The architecture of the Ouled el Hadef quarter of Tozeur
is typical of the Djerid region.
Buildings are faced with pale yellow sun-baked bricks made of sand and clay and set in geometric patterns
reminiscent of the motifs of Berber fabrics. Wooden doors are regularly given a fresh coat of blue or green paint.

In the Dahar mountains:

an elderly arabized Berber with his granddaughter in the village of Toujane.

The alleys of the oasis

Islam is both a religion and a way of life and, as such, is reflected in Saharan architecture. People's privacy is carefully safeguarded by a dense and intricate network of twists, turns and enclosures.

Terraces allow the women to spend time outdoors while remaining safe from public gaze. On the other hand, markets are held in the open air beyond the network of homes. The narrow and often tortuous alleyways represent a compromise between the two extremes. A stroll along them gives a good impression of the life that flourishes all around. Children shout and laugh in the alleyways, plates of couscous are carried from one house to the next, perfectly balanced on the head of a young girl, and veiled silhouettes laden with heavy baskets full of provisions pass slowly in front of you.

Left to right, top to bottom: Ghadames (Libya), Ghadames (Libya), Tozeur (Tunisia), Ghadames (Libya), Ghadames (Libya). Opposite: Tamentit (Algeria).

The *ksar* of Tamerza (opposite)
and the fortified barn of Ksar-Ouled-Soltane (above)

offer different forms of protection for their inhabitants.

The enclosures of the *ksar*, or fortified village, defend both those who live there

and their homes against attack, while the fortified barn or *ksour* is made up

of a honeycomb of cells on different levels (*ghorfas*),

overlooking a communal courtyard, and are used

to store the vital harvests upon which the locals depend.

Paradise does exist. If you need convincing, simply stroll through the gardens that surround most of the oases of the northern Sahara in Algeria, in the Saoura, M'Zab and Souf regions. A single well or spring is enough to bring the world to life. Growers constantly strive to maintain a crop rotation strategy, whereby vegetables, fruit trees and date palms are grown in turn. Tomatoes, carrots, salad, oranges, dates and figs fill the market stalls, manna that flourishes in the shelter of bushes, in the cool shade of the undergrowth and amid the scent of freshly cut grass. Palms, fig trees and bulrushes sway in the gentle wind. A sense of calm, even serene joy prevails in the haven of the oasis. It's like a desert version of an allegory of the Earthly Paradise, or Arcadia, with the oasis as the focal point.

This fine balance is resistant to changes in the order and scale of things. A profound sense of unity and harmony exists in the layout of the towns and villages surrounding the palm groves. In the Sahara, human habitat is inextricably linked with the oasis and the gardens that sustain life. This becomes keenly obvious when observed from the air, flying over Ghardaïa, El-Golea and El-Oued, whether by plane or in a hot air balloon.

To see the towns of M'Zab from a hot-air balloon is a rare privilege, especially when one takes to the skies from the market square, specially prepared for the purpose. Seconds after take-off the network of overlapping terraces, interior courtyards and narrow, winding streets becomes clear. The Mozabites brought to their habitat the relationship with religion that underpins their whole way of life. Like the Puritans, these descendants of a strict Muslim sect, banished from Hedjaz in the first century after the Hegira (the departure of the prophet Muhammad from Mecca, 622AD), gathered in a holy place and prepared for confrontation with orthodox groups. A concentric town was the result, all arteries of which converge on the main mosque, the houses on the outskirts forming a protective rampart.

In Souf the design of homes and streets is deliberately linear, whereas palm groves are oval in shape. Only the domed roofs, which are common, interrupt the straight lines of the houses, and curves remain exclusive to the gardeners' plots. Faced with the surrounding erg (sand sea), farmers had to choose between the constant effort to bring water to the surface (using manpower or beasts of burden) or greater proximity to the ground water itself. They chose the latter solution and hollowed out a series of basins, at the base of which dozens of palm trees are pampered into production. The maintenance of these **ghouts** (sunken palm groves) requires regular and rigorous care, not only must the trees be fertilized and their fruit harvested, but also the huge sand masses that can so easily engulf the palms must be routinely curbed. Hedges of palms act as local breakwaters, holding back the sand by forming a boundary beyond which unwanted sand is thrown, hence their more manageable circular .shape. Beyond these oases, the desert reasserts its rights and the ocean of sand stretches out towards the horizons, its waves of **barkhanes** (crescent-shaped dunes) and star-shaped dunes lashed by the winds like a semi-petrified thousand-year-old sea.

Opposite: in the gardens of In-Salah
Previous page: Souf

The western Sahara in Algeria is covered by ergs:
the Chech stretches as far as Mauritania and Mali and the Great Western Erg is so vast that it took Alain Sèbe
no fewer than three hours to fly across it during his aerial photography project.
Confronted by the ubiquitous and often menacing sand, oasis dwellers have come up with some ingenious ideas,
growing palm trees in the dune hollows (near Beni-Abbes, opposite) and building *ksars* in sheltered valleys (in the Saoura wadi, above)
or in the *sebkhas* (enclosed depressions) spared by the *barkhanes* (Timimoun *sebkha*, below).

Previous pages, left: The marketplace of Ghardaïa;
right: a *ksar* submerged by the Timimoun palm grove.

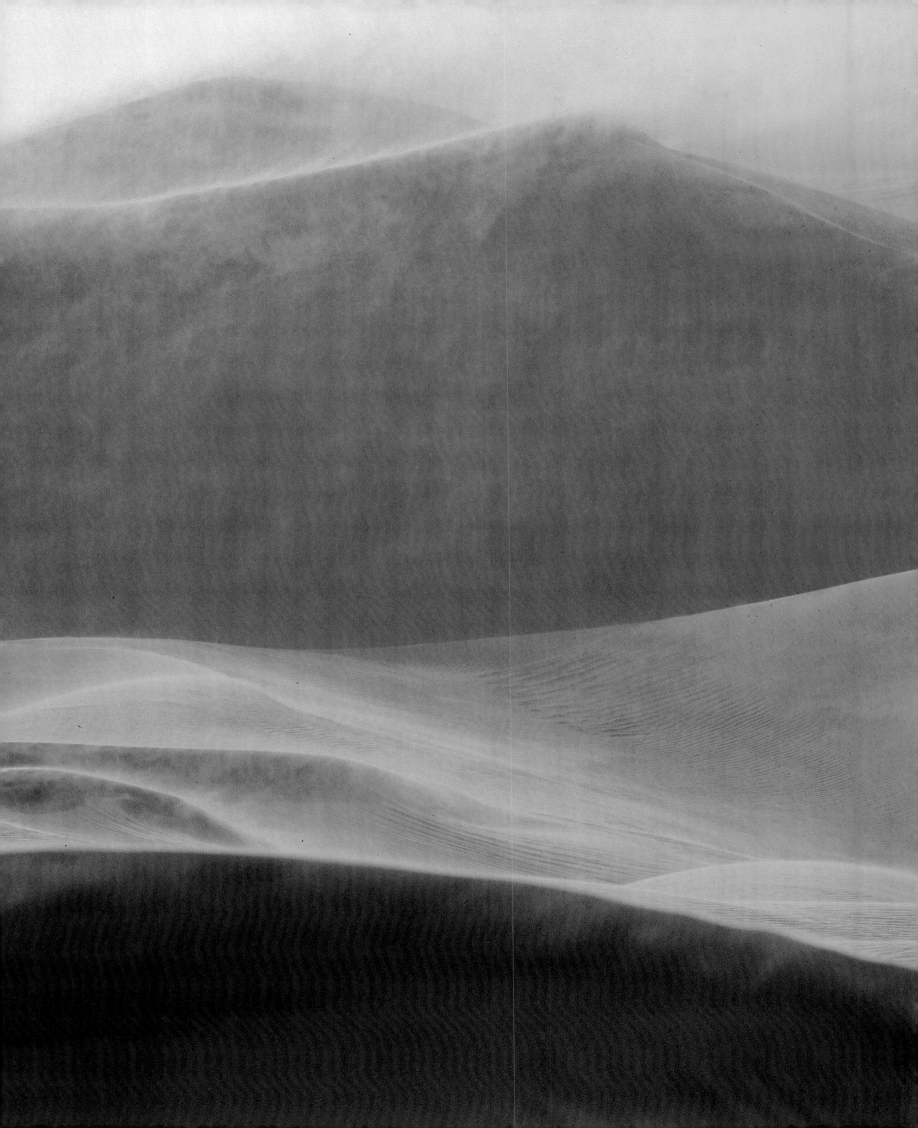

A *ghout* (tunnelled palm grove) in the Guemar region (Souf),
a green citadel encircled by the menacing dunes.
Two concentric hedges protect the palms and tiny gardens,
illustrating the cruel and endless battle within nature waged between sand and vegetation.

Previous pages: a windstorm near El-Golea.

This aerial view of Guemar shows the urban planning characteristic of the towns of Souf: straight alleys run parallel or at right angles to each other, heading north to south or west to east.

Houses have domed roofs and rooms arranged around large inner courtyards. Many private wells can be seen.

Overleaf: Ghardaïa.

A low flight over the town shows clearly the intricate network of houses

and the harmony of their blue- and white-painted walls.

In the land of Ilaman

Algeria

When the Amenokal (chief) of Hoggar, Moussa-ag-Amastane, was invited to Paris in 1910, he is said to have told his hosts confidently: 'It is true that France has the Eiffel Tower, but we, on the other hand, have Ilaman.' It is not Hoggar's highest peak – that distinction belongs to Tahat at 2,908m/9,540ft – but it has by far the greatest symbolic significance. When seen from Terhenanet, the village lying at the heart of Atakor, it looks like a huge pantheon, its features eroded by time. An open-air mosque, the **tamedjida** of Illaman, has been built nearby, its sober mihrab (niche or slab indicating the direction of Mecca) carved from layers of lava. This wind-lashed place of worship is a reflection of the Hoggar massif itself: impressive, unadorned, austere. In the summer it is comfortably cool but winter temperatures are by no means clement. In December, at an altitude of 2,728m/8,950ft, currents of air as cold as those from the Alps swirl around the hermitages of the Assekrem plateau, where the monks of the Petits Frères de Jésus continue the work of Charles de Foucauld.

Atakor, a jagged mountain around which steep-banked wadis or streams snake their way, is central to the lives of the Tuareg people in Hoggar. They learned how to survive in its inhospitable conditions and sought further afield for other essentials, but colonization put a stop to that process. The Tuaregs knew how to live on the bare minimum, being so familiar with their terrain that they could track down the merest scrap of edible vegetation, the least drops of moisture or trap the wariest moufflon. If danger threatened, they would barricade the main passes or, better still, organize an ambush. The second Flatters mission in 1881 experienced this response, being attacked and half-massacred in the In-Ouhaouen wadi by Tuaregs who wanted to put end the French threat and get their hands on the spoils. Such actions effectively dissuaded foreign enterprise until the battle of Tit in 1902, when the Tuaregs met their downfall and the flower of Kel-Ahaggar's warriors were cut down. This event had momentous repercussions in a society that so highly valued courage in combat. The people of Kel-Ahaggar were rapidly allied to the French troops and a relationship based on respect and trust was built, resulting for the French in a greater understanding of and increased accessibility to the country. The Tuaregs adapted to a way of life in which raids played no part but their panache remained intact.

When Alain Sèbe first went to Hoggar, he found descendants of these Tuaregs still living there, and djellabas and blue turbans still in evidence. Tamashek, the Tuareg language, was widely spoken, being more useful for finding out about nomadic journeys than discussing the latest things on television. The encampments moved around Atakor following the availability of pasture, with the bleating of goats, braying of camels and shouts of the shepherds forming a cacophonous melody. Under the combined pressures of menacing drought, expanding desert, political influences and herds of tourists, the fragile balance of the region has been threatened. The following images show life in the Ilaman country as it was lived thirty years ago.

Opposite: Dar Moulay festival
Previous page: the Atakor massif, at the foot of the Ilaman Peak, in Hoggar

During the 1970s Alain Sèbe made his way,

on foot or camelback, up the Hoggar massif.

He travelled slowly, following the course of the wadis (in the Tanget wadi, opposite),

watchful of the smallest details. He made a number of retreats on the Assekrem plateau (seen from a plane, above)

in hermitages belonging to the Petits Frères de Jésus (Little Brothers of Jesus),

the monks who continue the work begun by Charles de Foucauld,

known as 'the white marabout', who worked on his Tuareg-French glossary and dictionary there.

Around 25 miles northwest of Tamanrasset,
the village of Tit holds an annual festival
to commemorate a holy man named Moulay.
Dar Moulay attracts large numbers of Kel-Ahaggar Tuaregs,
who arrive by any means possible.
Four-wheel drive vehicles kick up thick clouds of sand and the camel trails heave.
Those who are poorer but no less proud
crowd along the tracks to the village.

A *tagella* is a corn waffle

that is as easily prepared while travelling as outside the tent or under shelter (opposite: in Terhenanet).

Kneaded in a *tamenast* (a flat copper dish),

the paste is then cooked in the sand, steaming from the embers of a large fire.

The *tagella* is then broken up on a plate and sprinkled with butter and tomato sauce,

to make a delicious and satisfying meal.

For some, the Assekrem plateau is simply a wonderful panoramic viewpoint,
for others it is a place of pilgrimage.
Imbued with history, it is a stunning viewpoint over Atakor.

Turn your gaze from the hermitage built in 1910 by Charles de Foucauld
and face the most famous mountains of the Hoggar massif.
In one panorama, you will see the organ-like basalt peaks of Tezouyeg and Souinan (in the foreground),
the table-mass of In-Taraïn (to the left) and the solitary peak of Adedou (right, in the background).

Camel racing is one of the activities
that still demonstrates the fierce spirit and pride of the Tuareg people.
As can be seen from the start,
a race is no gentle affair as participants confront each other with symbolic,
proud gestures (opposite and above, in the Sersouf wadi, near Tamanrasset).
The rank and standing of each team
is indicated by the colour of the dromedary's coat,
the quality of saddle and crop and the attire and equipment of the riders,
who can be seen adjusting their headgear or *tagelmoust* seconds before the race commences.
These things count for as much as the final result.

In 1974, the Hoggar camps (in the Ilaman wadi, above)

    still reflected the ethnological divisions of the period between the wars.

The tent fabric, called *aukoum*, was made of animal skins stitched together,

    and the nomads would shelter under matting or *essaber*, made of *afezzou* (grass stems).

Now, both have virtually disappeared, being replaced by the canvas sheets

    and adobe structures of the settled nomads.

A reunion at the Taguemart camp: Alain Sebe arrives,
accompanied by an old friend with connections to the neighbouring Agouh-n-Tehlé tribe.

Overleaf: lengthy discussions take place
during the Dar Moulay festival.

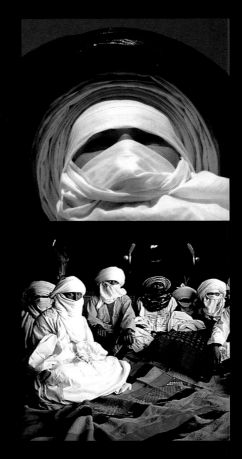

Veiled identity

The veil worn by Tuareg men acts as a form of identity card, and the manner in which the tagelmoust is wrapped around the head is an indicator of class.

The **tagelmoust**, known to the Arabs as a **litham**, is an indigo-coloured head wrap, as shiny as carbon paper. Imported from Nigeria at great expense, it is worn only on special occasions, such as traditional festivals, births, marriages (opposite, a Kel-Ajjer bridegroom) or the rare procession. However, over several decades an important change has taken place and a more practical, less fragile and less expensive turban, known as the **cheche**, has replaced the **tagelmoust** as standard headwear. White, black or khaki in colour, it is an Arab import. The relaxation of previously strictly enforced rules as to the visibility of men's mouths means that today some Tuaregs unveil the lower part of their faces.

Left to right, top to bottom: a Kel-Ahaggar Tuareg, a Kel-Ahaggar Tuareg, Kel-Ajjer Tuaregs, Kel-Ajjer Tuaregs, a Kel-Ajjer Tuareg, a Kel-Ahaggar Tuareg. Opposite: a Kel-Ajjer Tuareg.

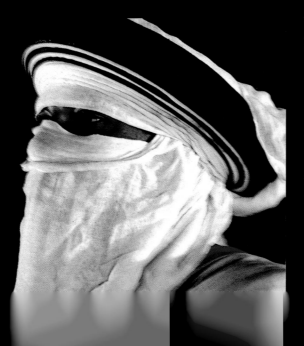

Nature, the architect
Algeria

Like the Libyan desert, the Hoggar Tassili, located in the extreme south of Algeria, is a region where nomads rarely settle. Most Tuaregs merely traverse it. In the late 1970s Saharan enthusiasts decided to explore it rather than simply crossing it. After several years spent in the oases of central Sahara, exploring the Hoggar massif and the plateaux of Ajjers, Alain Sèbe could not resist the lure of this little known region. It is made up of a series of sandstone plateaux, the residues of a sedimentary layer thrown up by lava in the Pleistocene era that formed Hoggar. The **tassilis** belong to a more extensive range that forms a 270-degree barrier, beginning at the Ahnet massif in the west and ending in the east with the last foothills of Ajjers. On their western and southern slopes the boundless, flat expanses of Tanezrouft, Tamesna and Ténéré begin.

The easiest route to the Tagrera wadi, one of the most varied of **tassilis**, begins at Tamanrasset. After leaving Hoggar, a monotonous, sandy plain gives way to the Ti-n-Tezedjnet pass with potentially spectacular views. Somehow, however, the vastness of the area renders the panorama at once visually astonishing and emotionally unengaging, like a masterpiece kept under glass. Closer scrutiny reveals the web of polished hills and outcrops like castles or cathedrals that lies in the far distance. But these reliefs in the landscapes remain distant; there are challenges to be confronted first. Alain Sebe undertook the discovery of this region in two ways, each silent: on foot and by hot-air balloon. To discover an environment on foot is to become intimate with its lines, perspectives and movements of light and dark, which play on the senses. Shadows dart on the narrow natural corridors, each step brings the sharp echo of pebbles or the dull crunch of gravel underfoot. Details are highlighted: wind-sculpted sandstone or grasses that have fought to survive in the shelter of a rocky cleft. The slightest change in the temperature affects the senses – the sudden brush of cooler air in the shadow of a massif or the surprisingly soft caress of the of the sand on the summit of small dunes. The relationship is less directly physical when travelling by a hot-air balloon but it affords a different perspective upon the landscape. Lines lengthen, shadows deepen, the Im-Meskor barrier stands boldly against the horizon. The balloon glides softly with the wind as views change and dimensions deepen. The landscape lies both at your feet and beyond your view.

Your gaze darts among the peaks of the massif not yet eroded by time and wind. Whipped by the storms, grains of sand take their toll on the sandstone. The wind is fiercer at ground level, given greater force by the funnel-shaped mounds of sand, and it whittles the base of the rocks, forming stone mushrooms. The wind's invisible hand works tirelessly, eroding and polishing the landscape, using eddies and swirls as its tools. Nature, the invisible architect, is hard at work in the **tassilis**.

Opposite: Hoggar Tassili: In-Tehog
Previous page: Hoggar Tassili: Tahaggart

The unusual shapes of the Laouni *tassilis* (above)

and those of El-Ghessour (opposite)

resemble petrified tree trunks or chess pieces.

Whether seen from the air, on foot or through a lens, they capture the imagination of all.

Overleaf: Hoggar Tassili: In-Tehog.

The acacia bush conceals a well.

Formed from sandstone,
of which it is the residue, sand invades the smallest chinks in the *tassili* massifs
(above: Ti-n-Akacheker in the Tagrera wadi).

The relationship between that which has already been pulverized by the wind

and that which will be crushed is part of the endless cycle of the desert.

The *tassilis* (opposite: Tagrera and above: Ti-m-Missao)
come in so many different forms, huge or compact,
in pieces or intact,
that their combinations are inexhaustible,
posing the question of whether they are rocks thrown at random on the sand
or silhouettes deliberately positioned on the dunes.

The 'red hour' in Tahaggart.
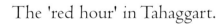
The sun's last rays are the call to make a halt
and take shelter from the cold night at the base of a rock.

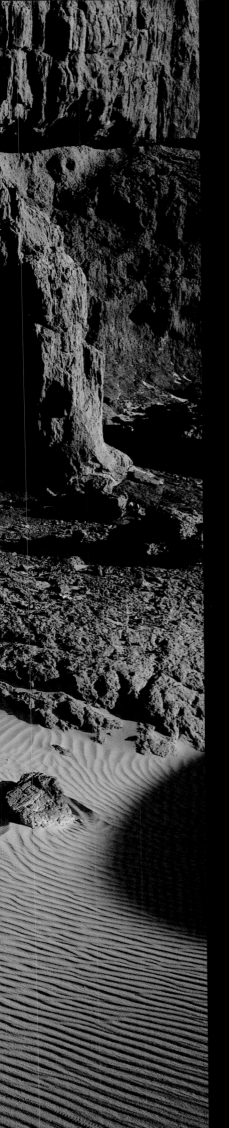

All it takes for a tree to root and grow

in the mineral-rich soil of the Ti-m-Missao *tassili* (above and opposite)

is a few drops of moisture

and a single seed blown there by the currents of air.

One tree, two images:

behind the camera, the eye watches.

The wind rakes the sand like an experienced gardener.

Wind and erosion form ripple marks on the sand,
creating a zen garden in the desert.

The domain of the Ajjers Tuaregs
Algeria

The domain of the Ajjers Tuaregs

The skies were venting their anger on the Admer plain, not far from Djanet. The very worst kind of wind whipped up the canvas and sent it crashing against the roll bar of the buffeted Toyota. Squalls flayed the windscreen, sand invaded the car and filled our nostrils. During a sudden sunny moment a caravan of camels appeared, forming a long, straggling black trail ahead. Two camel drivers led the procession, its mysterious, enigmatic air underlined by the inhospitable conditions. Behind them dark stains on the ground caught our eye: a herd of goats following in the camels' wake. We stopped and waited as the shapes became clearer, then descended from the vehicle to approach the small group. Around thirty animals were slowly moving forward, led by their shepherd. Far from any well or pasture, the man and his flock formed an indivisible unit. The animals made no attempt to run away and yet we wondered how they would survive in this environment rich in minerals but not in water.

The Tassili N'Ajjers is a world of ergs, plains, escarpments, gorges and wadis, as large as France. Only a few villages can be discerned in this environment where nomads roam until drought consumes the vegetation and their livelihood. The network of trails links the various settlements, surrounded by huge areas abandoned when the sources of water dried up. Paradoxically, the Ajjers is the scene of one of the Sahara's most lively festivals, the Sebiba, held each year by those who struggle for survival in this sterile landscape. This Dantesque environment, strewn with piles of rocks, sterile ergs and windswept plains, has forced man to retreat into its canyons, tiny wadis and depressions. Yet encampments strike up once more as soon as rain falls on the area. The grass grows quickly and lasts longer. Tents and villages spring up in response to the universal instinct for self-preservation and protection, as they seek shelter and comfort.

Colonial invasion divided the land of the Ajjers Tuaregs, which stretches beyond the Tassili frontiers to embace part of Fezzan. It extends from the Algeria–Libya border, covering over 620 miles from Amguid to the Adjal wadi. Despite the rivalry that has often broken out within the tribes themselves, the Kel-Ajjer maintains a strong group spirit, forged in the struggles with the Hoggar Tuaregs. Local tales celebrate brave, warlike exploits, stories that owe more to imaginative spontaneity than to historical accuracy. The yarns are often spun after a couscous shared under the shelter of a tent or **zeriba** (reed hut).

Alain Sèbe's memories of the Ajjers are among his fondest in the Sahara: flocks and herds setting off at dawn amid a cacophony of bleats and bellows, wonderful hospitality in forgotten villages deep in secret valleys, impromptu invitations to wedding ceremonies, festivities and negotiations, accompanied day and night by melodic drumming, and **meharees** held on the plains or in the shelter of canyons. His aesthetic senses were certainly fired by such experiences, but at the same time he enjoyed immersing himself in the daily lives of the Kel-Ajjer people, for whom he felt both deep friendship and great respect.

Opposite: Admer plain
Previous page: the Timras ('molars' in Tamashek)

The Arabs call the crest of a dune a *sif*,

which translates literally as a sabre.

When the light settles on the dune (as here in the Tihodaïne erg),

the sharp edges look like the ferocious blade

of a *yataghan* (long curved sword).

Four camel drivers and around twenty camels navigate the ocean of sand.

Some of the animals carry the vital forage for the caravan.

While Arabs drive their camels in a single line, the Tuaregs lead them in rows.

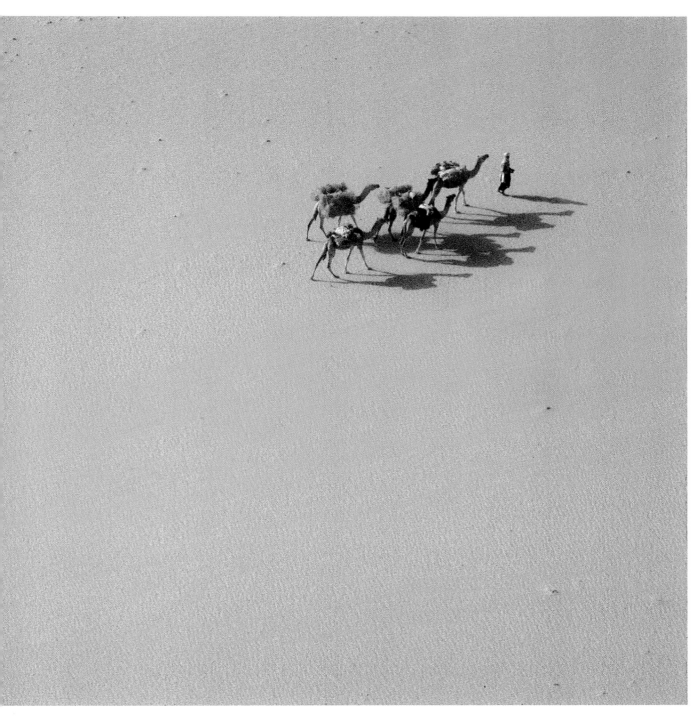

Caravan drivers need little to help them navigate, using features in the landscape to orient themselves, such as mountains, peaks and plateaux together with *redjens* (cairns), the colour of the sand, the orientation of the *nebkhas* (sandy hillocks) and the stars or constellations. Young people begin acquiring this skill from their first caravan journey, aged around fifteen. Participation marks the transition from child to adult, a progression sealed by the donning of the veil.

The Tadrart, part of the Tassili N'Ajjers region,

is the result of a political division between Algeria and Libya.

In 1919, an arbitrary line was drawn that put an end to Franco–Italian antagonism.

The Ti-n-Meerzouga erg (above) in Algeria

is the extension of the Iguidi Oua-n-Kasa of Libya.

Erosion in Tadrart is fierce;
whipped up by the wind the sand attacks the sandstone massifs,
forming astonishing anthropomorphic shapes.

At dusk,

when the shadows lengthen and colours turn deep bronze,

the **wadis of the Tassili N'Ajjers** are a pleasant rest-spot (above: the Tililine wadi).

Travellers halt their camels or vehicles and set up camp,

and Tuaregs sit around the ethel trees, mulling over the events of the day.

Opposite: the Imessouan wadi.

A green carpet springs up at the first rainfall or flood,

and the nomads take immediate advantage of it.

In 1991, Dahmane, Alain's guide,

suspected that an encampment had sprung up in the pasturage of the Ihane wadi (opposite).

Bleatings, bellowings and brayings amid the clusters of vegetation confirmed his intuition,

and the crowing of a cock soon signalled where the tents had been erected.

The sedentary villages are more peaceful (above, in the Aharhar wadi)

and settlers lead their lives according to a different rhythm,

one not dictated by the perpetual search for pasture.

The tea ceremony

Green tea was unknown in the Sahara until the early twentieth century but it has been incorporated into the way of life since and a sort of 'tea etiquette' quickly established itself.

Teapots gently hiss on the hot coals. Two pots, a few glasses, a sugar loaf, a handful of tea and some water are all that is required for the correct entertainment of one's guests. Depending upon availability, mint or a few strands of aromatic herbs harvested from the wadi are added and much appreciated. Tea is both an excuse and a catalyst for conversation, and there is a strict code of conduct for its consumption. One of the best-known traditions is the three glasses rule. Woe betide a guest who drinks the first glass of tea but declines the rest – this is seen by his hosts as an offensive gesture.

Left to right, top to bottom: tea-time in the Ajjers (Algeria), the Ajjers (Algeria), Acacous (Libya), Saoura (Algeria). Opposite: in Moorish country.

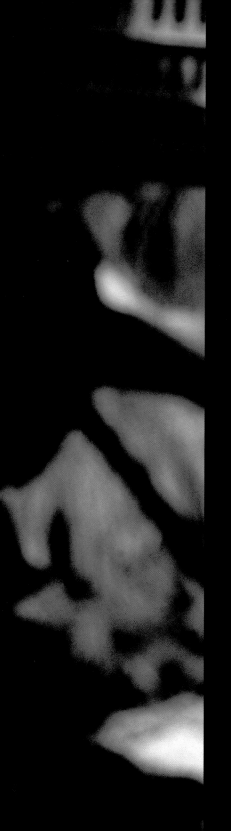

Tuareg women enjoy great freedom,
as demonstrated by the uncovered face of this Kel-Ajjer woman (opposite).

After marriage, women retain substantial independence
and hold on to their possessions throughout their lives.

The husband is responsible for supporting the household,

and thus a woman's means can increase.

Her servants, on the other hand, are not afforded the same level of respect

(above, a shepherdess in the Tadjeradjeri wadi).

Form and function

Despite their traditional contempt for any form of manual labour, high-ranking Tuareg women enjoy spending time making beautiful wooden utensils.

Working in wood is seen as less demeaning than working on the land. Using adzes, the women patiently make milking vessels, wooden bowls, pestles, funnels and pulleys for wells. They fashion delicately woven baskets from rough esparto grass found in the wadi and are skilled at working with animal skin and make goatskin water carriers, vital for survival in the desert (opposite). The manufacture of more complicated equipment and tools is the exclusive domain of the enaden (men from the artisan classes), including camel saddles (below, right, a woman's saddle ready for assembly) or red copper bowls (below, left, a tamenast). In addition, the men chisel tent pegs and wooden utensils.

Left to right, top to bottom: Terhenanet (Algeria), Tissalatine wadi (Algeria), Gabr'Aoun (Libya), Adrar Ahnet (Algeria), Adrar Ahnet (Algeria), Adrar Ahnet (Algeria). Opposite: Aharhar wadi (Algeria).

Pre-Pharaonic Sahara

Algeria and Libya

When Rameses II was building the sculptures of Abu Simbel, the Neolithic artists of the Sahara had long since completed their masterpieces, begun way back in 6,000 BC. During that period, the Sahara enjoyed a much kinder climate than today and cave art reflects this luxuriance. When the drought arrived, the artists chronicled its course. Sheltered under rocks, huddled amid erratic blocks, on stones polished by ice or lashed by storms, these early artists faithfully reproduced what they saw or remembered. Their work forms an astonishing encyclopedia of animals, from powerful predators to pelicans. Daily activities of human life – hunting and toiling – are charted in detail. Images recount the story of the Sahara, clearly depicting its transition from lush grass to golden but sterile sand. It is a profound and startling testimony to the Saharan world six thousand years before the Christian era. Four different periods are distinguishable.

Some now dried-up wadis display images of animals that once grazed there, a range as wide and varied as that found today in Africa's national parks. Rhinos, hippos, crocodiles, elephants, lions, giraffes, antelopes and ostriches were among the favourite subjects of the carvers at work between the 6th and 4th centuries BC, known as the 'Bubaline' period, after the buffalo (**Bubalus antiquus**, now extinct in the region). The Djerat wadi in Ajjers and the valleys that encroach upon the Messak Settafet in Fezzan are among the key areas of this period.

It was probably around the same time that the mysterious frescoes known collectively as the 'Round Heads' were painted. The simplified contours and elongated, featureless, rounded heads suggested to some that they depicted extra-terrestrials. Paintings from the 'Bovidian' era (4th–2nd century BC) feature herders, their families and their flocks. Red ochre is the most commonly used colour and these highly realistic paintings are masterpieces of precision, balance and harmony.

As water became increasingly scarce, herders gave place to hunter-gatherers and the art became more stylized, with heads being conveyed in a simple line. Hunting scenes appeared, complete with bows, axes and clubs, seeming to denote a more hostile environment. Corresponding to the arrival of horses in North Africa, horse images then entered the frame in a period consequently known as 'Caballine' or the 'horse period' (2nd–1st century BC).

The precursors of camels can be seen in some paintings of the period known as 'Camelline', which emerged just before the Christian era. The tendency towards simplification becomes more accentuated and obvious, to the point of graffiti. However some remarkable images depict a way of life quite similar to that of Tuaregs today – scenes show figures riding upon saddled dromedaries, hunting and using a variety of javelins, bordered with **tifinar** characters (Berber script using only consonants) that are still in use today.

Left: Tassili N'Ajjers, the Ta-n-Zoumaïtak cave
Previous page: around El-Hassi in Libya

Niches in the rocks of the Sahara harbour art
that testifies to the extremely close relationship between painting
and the surface on which the artists worked.

Neolithic artists did not have the luxury of a flat canvas and clearly defined limits.
Their compositions are enriched by the exigencies of the rock
and of the grainy, curved, textured surface on which they are painted.
Ochre and kaolin are used here to depict a pastoral scene
from the Bovidian era
(Opposite: Tascomamal, North Tibesti: 90 x 90cm/35½ x 35½ in).

The skill of **Neolithic artists** at rock chiselling and engraving matches their talent at painting.

Engravings preceded painting in the Sahara and can be found in many locations from the Atlantic to the Nile.

Technique, style and patina vary between regions but the themes remain constant,

with a common interest in fauna (opposite, a group of giraffes in the El-Galhien wadi in Fezzan: 210 x 150cm/83 x 59in).

The same subjects were depicted either in fine, deep and polished engravings

(below, a Tirarmatine bubal in the Djerat wadi, in Ajjers: 120 x 125cm/47 x 49in)

or in a simpler execution (above, a group of three giraffes in the Ghari wadi,

to the south of the Ajjers plateau: 290 x 230cm/114 x 91in).

A herd of cattle (bovids)
sketched in the Tihaharen wadi in Fezzan (left, 80 x 90cm/32 x 35in).
Certain differences in the patina of the ochre suggest that this depiction of livestock
was completed in several stages.

By contrast, there is a striking sense of unity in this image of
an archer painted on the walls of a shelter in Jabbaren
(above, Tassili N'Ajjers, 15 x 22cm/6 x 9in),
and the pure lines have all the elegance of archaic Greek athletes.
It is a fine portrayal of a proud figure
and one of the great masterpieces of Saharan cave art.

The Tassili N'Ajjers (right, a rock shelter in Ti-n-Tazarift,
showing a fresco measuring 150 x 180 cm/59 x 71in) is a veritable open-air museum,
like that of Messak Settafet in Libya.
You would be fortunate to find the paintings at first glance, being more likely
to happen upon them in crevices after hours of walking, sometimes under a leaden sky.
The richness of such discoveries forms a remarkable contrast
with the drought-ridden environment.

Travellers who have done their research
will know that the low, dry-stone walls that symbolically protect most of the shelters in the Tassili N'Ajjers
already existed when the cave paintings were discovered in the 1930s.
Perhaps they testify to the respect inspired by these remarkable works,
which are worthy of inclusion among the world's finest artworks.

Ti-n-Aboteka in the Tassili N'Ajjers (above, left).

The use of different techniques in Saharan rock paintings has caused much debate and controversy among archaeologists.

However, the gradual progression from naturalism to schematization

has been generally accepted.

The figures with long headdresses and the cattle (left, 135 x 225cm/53 x 89in);

derive from the 'round head' style, a unique combination of realism and symbolism.

Two Negroid archers (above, centre, 170 x 170cm/67 x 67in)
demonstrate the highly realistic style characteristic of the artists of the Bovidian period.
The appearance of the horse heralded a more schematized style.
This cart in full gallop (above, right, 50 x 65cm/20 x 26in)
comes from the Caballine period and shows how realism was sacrificed
in order to convey movement.

Although the appearance of the camel in rock paintings coincided with an eventual stylistic deterioration, some of the images still have significant aesthetic value.

This is certainly the case with this elegant depiction of a dromedary, discovered in Oua-n-Bender in the Tassili N'Ajjers.
Its modest dimensions (20 x 20cm/8 x 8in) add to its delicacy.

An everyday scene,

as depicted by the artists of Tamadjert, in the Tassili N'Ajjers (30 x 30cm/12 x 12in).

The two women are carrying a heavy object – perhaps a sack, vessel or gourd –

and the third figure is painted in different shades of ochre,

with simple kaolin strokes representing the three bracelets worn on the left arm.

As in other works from the Caballine period, the heads are stick-like.

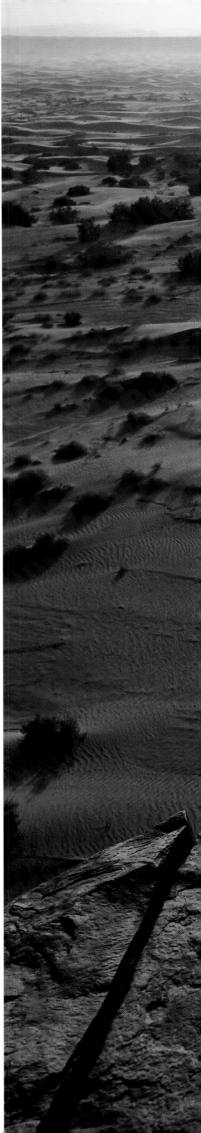

A sudden encounter
with traces of our distant forbears
is a frequent delight for the Saharan traveller.

During his search for a vantage point from which to view
the first line of the Oubari *edeyen* in Fezzen, Libya, Alain Sèbe made his way up a rocky outcrop,
fighting a strong wind that had been blowing since the previous day.
On reaching the platform,
he made his way to what he instinctively felt was the best viewing point,
at the edge of which he found
tracks left by travellers from the distant past.
The sandals are carved life size.

Stones, sand and water

Libya

Fezzan covers a remarkably large area, about the size of France, and is one of three historic regions in Libya, together with Tripolitania to the north and Cyrenaica to the east. Rocky plateaux or hammadas stretch towards the horizon, seemingly endless carpets of stones and rocks. Vast ergs, such as the **edeyens** (rounded dunes) of Oubari or Murzuk, encompass millions of cubic feet of sand. Sometimes, lakes lie in the hollows of the dunes, surrounded by gently swaying palm trees and bulrushes, oases that welcome and enchant the traveller lucky enough to find them. A journey to Fezzan offers few interesting interludes to punctuate the empty canvas stretching to the skyline and the long, straight, interminable roads. Mile upon empty mile (hundreds in all) challenge one's concentration, but the few, intermittent villages do have interesting features, such as the attractive traditional architecture of Ghadamès and El-Fogaha. The vast 'no man's land' that lies between each stop makes the traveller all the more appreciative on arrival at a settlement. No fewer than 500 miles of rocky land lie between Tripoli and Sebha, the main town in the Fezzan region, and a journey along the endless road is nature's own exercise in sensory deprivation.

The Adjal wadi is a welcome sight for any traveller, who is then further cheered by the lush green gardens and bright red tomatoes in the ensuing villages. The **edeyen** of Oubari in the background catches the final rays of the sun, the dunes turning a deep, burnished bronze and the shadows almost violet. Seconds later, the first of the street lamps light up like garlands along the way, giving the simple palm huts the air of beach cabins. Smoke rises from braziers where lamb chops and kebabs gently sizzle. Furtive shadows sometimes glide along the road, cars whose faint sidelights can barely be seen. Some made fortunes during the air embargo imposed against Libya between 1992 and 1999, but for others it accelerated the existing decline, as the Toyota of our guide Omar, with whom we travelled in 1996, testified. It had negotiated the desert dunes for 20 years, its bodywork ricocheting to the convulsions of the engine and its wheels buffeted by every mound of sand. The scarcity of spare parts made maintenance impossible. However, Omar excelled in all things to do with balance, both of temperament and mechanics, although his skill at keeping us upright and his 'shortcuts' across the ridges often brought those who followed in his tracks out in a cold sweat.

Gabr'Aoun lake appeared suddenly in a corridor between the dunes, reflecting the wall of sand that surrounds it. The spot is too perfect to escape the overworked category of cliché: the almost miraculous lake was a haven of peace, only a gentle breeze blowing over its waters and the soft swish of palm leaves interrupted a velvet silence. However all this changed on the following day, its perfection suddenly shattered when a cruel wind blew sand like a rain of needles into our eyes. Dust whipped up and launched a ferocious attack on us as we lay in our sleeping bags, drying skin, chapping lips, filling the eyes with sticky grit and shrivelling our fingers as the dry wind cracked the pages of the crumpled logbook. In the Sahara, as elsewhere, the wind brings both rain and good weather.

Opposite: Oum-el-Mâ lake
Previous page: Tadrart-Acacous, in the In-Dinen massif

A scene captured in the *edeyen* of **Murzuk**
one February morning shows clusters of *drinn* (wild grass) catching the rays of the rising sun
and forming a subtle paint palette of browns.

This meagre vegetation in the heart of the dune
demonstrates the fleeting but endlessly renewed cycle of growth and decay in this mineral-rich world.

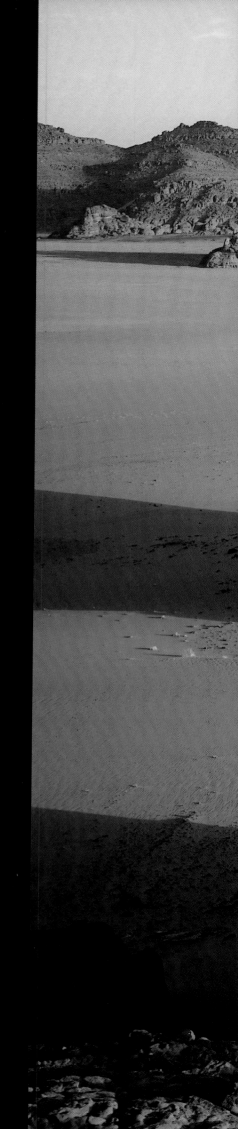

Wind, flood, ice and sea ...

During the course of its history, erosion in the Sahara has had many agents,
some of which are hard to imagine, given the present-day features of the landscape.
It is perhaps more worrying
that the sandstone that is slowly decomposing today
(opposite: Tihaharen wadi; above: Fozzigiaren wadi)
is shedding sediment carried there three hundred million years ago
by the very same agents.

In the midst of the arid landscape that surrounds them (above),
the lakes of the Ramlat Daouada (opposite: Oum-el-Mâ)
appear like small patches of paradise.
However, those who lived there until 1987 in a state of almost total autonomy
were no strangers to terrible hardship.
They survived by growing sorghum and a few vegetables,
supplementing their diet with dates, edible algae and lakeside plankton.
Artemia salina — small worms harvested by the women — formed an important part of their daily intake,
and the Arabs were quick to dub them the *Daouada* — the men of worms.

The barren landscape, rich in minerals but little else,
that lies at the heart of Acacous: only the *inselbergs* (outcrops),
like a petrified sea of sand and sandstone, interrupt the monotony
of the plateau stretching towards the horizon.

In many ways the Acacous region is similar to the Hoggar *tassilis*.
The cirque that lies within the remains of the eroded rock in the Tiharen wadi
(opposite) symbolizes the limitless choices
and possibilities that confront the desert traveller.
The wind whistles through the nooks and crannies of this natural maze,
fallen rocks hinder progress as the sandstone crumbles underfoot.
Such practical difficulties add a little spice to the discovery of this untamed environment.

Above: the vast expanses of the Hammada-el-Hamrah.

Due to the lack of vegetation,

the geological formation of Saharan rock

is exposed to the elements and visible to the naked eye.

Nature has done much of the geologists' work for them.

The upper layer of rock on this outcrop in

the Hammada-el-Hamrah is considerably sturdier than the one below

and is therefore more resistant to the assaults of various types of erosion.

On the other side of the horizon
Libya

Tmissah is a small, sleepy town that marks the end of the road. Wind rattles the creaking doors of the shack near the abandoned service station and the stillness of the streets around will not be broken until the sand ebbs away. This is the last oasis before Koufra, 500 miles on the other side of the endless reg and erg. One longs for an even half-open café in which to enjoy a last glass of tea before desert sand fills the nostrils. This is the departure point for one of the Libyan Sahara's two volcanoes, the Ouaou-en-Namous. A crater of modest dimensions embedded in the sand of the surrounding plain, it's quite easy to miss, but it would be a real shame to do so, for it is one of the jewels of the desert. Its edges sculpt impressive curves, the grey sand dunes describe dramatic, sweeping arabesques and the volcanic cone presents a smooth silhouette on one side, a jagged cliff on the other. Dense clusters of reed form azure reflections on the lakes that are home to splashing water birds. The light pinpoints the different textures: the glittering sheets of water, the dull black of volcanic ash, the vibrant sparkling of the **guezbas** (small reeds) and the lacy texture of the gullies of the cone. The tones range from deep sapphire to slate grey as the time and conditions vary.

The view from the top of the volcanic cone rolls out endlessly before you, gently sloping towards a horizon disappearing into the distant mist. It is like being on a deserted island in the middle of the ocean, the round edges of the world sketched out ahead. The sandy plain seems to heave under a heavy swell. Navigation here is easy by compass or by GPS (unusable elsewhere because of the hilly terrain). Towards the east and the south, travellers simply point the steering wheel at the straight line that traverses the vast regs of the Tibesti and Kalanshio **serirs** (flat plains) that divide the world of the Toubous to the south from that of the Egyptians to the east. The uninterrupted, flat plain stretches out on all sides and the road continues monotonously ahead, deviating neither to the right nor the left, traversing neither hill nor valley. The desert is bounded by the **serir**, which may be rocky or sandy, honed and polished by the winds, as uniform and almost as comfortable as any tarmac road. A car is indispensable in this region but the unchanging view, identical ahead as behind, can make a driver sleepy. The monotony of the engine noise lulls the mind and depresses the mood, while the soporific, lengthy journey makes the legs swell uncomfortably. Bright blue sky and sun-drenched sandy plains encircle you, and every cloud is a welcome diversion in this universe where the horizon retreats as quickly as you advance.

Thoughts turn to the great challenges and heroic feats of the past, when caravans cut through one mirage to the next, week after week, using a narrow **mejdbed** (camel track) or merely the shadow of their own animals to determine the route. The team had to be self-sufficient, carrying all they could possibly need, including bundles of forage for the camels. One can imagine the slow, determined pace of the camel drivers, set by centuries of adaptation to the desert, their repetitive chants fading into the emptiness of the encircling, hostile world.

Opposite: the Ouaou-en-Namous volcano
Previous double page: an acacia stranded in the
last lava flows of Haroudj-el-Assouad.

The volcanic cone of Ouaou-en-Namous

is so engulfed by its own ashes that it is visible only

from the edge of the crater.

In the foreground lie the sodium crystal lakes, surrounded by small reeds (*guezbas*).

The peaks of the Bab Djebel (above and opposite)

stand sentinel-like on the sandy plain,

heralding the imminent Tibesti massif.

During the recent clashes between Chad and Libya

tanks passed nearby.

The contours of Tibesti form an almost perfect Y-shape,
its eastern flank lying mostly within Libyan territory.
The Toubous nomads of the region differentiate between the two slopes
according to the direction in which the waters of the *enneris* (wadis) flow –
the eastwards flow is the Ouri Djebel
whereas the Dohone Djebel runs to the west.

As in the rest of the Tibesti range, the rocks here present a black and shiny appearance.

Above: Tong wadi (Oued Tong) in Ouri

Despite frequent conflicts in the region,
some Toubous families
continue to live near the border.

(Opposite: a hut in the Tascomamal wadi near Chad)

Their survival depends both upon their small herds of goats and on government aid,

and their lifestyle stands in stark contrast to the riches of antiquity

derived from the amazonstone deposits of Zouma (above),

embedded in the lower foothills of Tibesti.

To the east of El-Gatroun (previous double page),
a perfect example of the vast, limitless spaces in east Libya, known as the *serir* of Kalanshio (or Serir Tibesti).
The sandy plain is completely flat, devoid of even the slightest relief,
in the final stage of the erosion process.

Above: the Ouri djebel
in the Tong wadi (Oued Tong).

Men, women and children prepare the camels for their journey to Chad.
Blankets, teapots and cooking pots have been packed in the bags.
After several hours of frenetic activity
the village will fall silent once more as the caravan departs.

Signs of life spring from the sporadic breaches of the otherwise barren horizon.
In El Fogaha (opposite) both humans and palm trees
seek shelter against the winds that sweep across the reg.
The *ksar* (not shown) is built on the slopes of the valley whose floor supports
the carefully maintained gardens.

On the other hand,
the Ouaou-en-Namous (above)
appears never to have been settled for long,
despite the evidence of the remains of *zeribas*.
Nevertheless palm trees and reeds thrive around
the brackish water of the lakes.

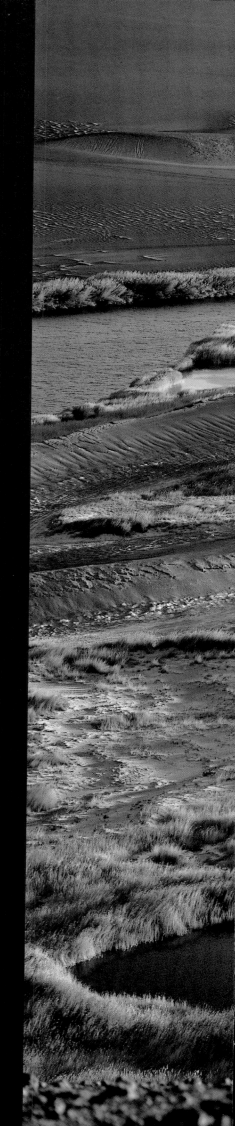

'This cruel land can cast a spell which no temperate clime can match.'

T.E. LAWRENCE

Opposite: the Ouaou-en-Namous volcano

A barren plateau, an enchanted valley

Egypt

It was not until the early 20th century that cartographers were finally able to complete the maps of Egypt. Only committed explorers ventured beyond the banks of the Nile but to leave behind the oases of the Libyan desert for what the French called the 'desert of Bedoa' was almost an adventure too far. The fear was less of dangerous encounters than of the lack of landmarks, oases and places in which to find fresh supplies en route. To the west of Farafra or Dakhla, the 'Great Sea of Sand', an endless backbone of dunes, unfurls. It is said that here in 525BC a raging storm engulfed the Persian army of the King of Kings, Cambyses II, despatched to conquer the Ammon oasis, now known as Siouah.

The barrier of the Libyan desert isolates the Gilf Kebir plateau from the rest of the world. In order to reach it travellers must traverse vast, empty expanses or navigate their way over hills of sand, layered like onion rings by a capricious, unpredictable wind. No cooling, thirst-quenching water awaits them on arrival their destination. This corner of the world is rough and hostile, punctuated by a few valleys where a handful of acacia bushes are slowly strangled by drought. The recognition of the vast distances to be covered simply to get here, or to return, adds to its inhospitable, even hostile aspect. Not much survives in these parts, and it is hard to imagine that even a major downpour could bring any real colour to the place. Only the bare, polished skulls of moufflons remain and long-since empty wells have silted up with sand. A scattering of trees still cling to life while others have already given up the struggle and surrendered to dust.

Despite the inauspicious welcome, there is an enigmatic, almost inexplicable allure to the region. A satellite can easily pinpoint its location, but even the most sophisticated technology would fail to define its real character and convey the effect of its almost monastic silence and the lengthening, haunting shadows. A mixture of admiration tinged with fear colours the idea of this dry, arid land that stretches to engulf the north of Sudan, in Ash-Shimaliyya.

Like the Persian soldiers before them, modern explorers reached the Libyan desert from the river Nile. Our own itinerary follows the route in reverse, to Aswan. The valley of the Nile suddenly rises up behind our dusty windscreen, unannounced and unexpected. Thin ribbons of vegetation line the river on both sides, easily absorbed by the sand and rocks that surround them. Life is focussed around the water's edge, reluctant to leave the valley that is protected from the warm winds of the desert. Our sudden return to civilization is accompanied by the return of temporarily suspended concerns. Clouds of insects buzzing around our heads take the place of the odd fly or dragonfly. The sheer size and regularity of the Nile astonishes as we travel in a felucca, not on a sea of sand but on water.

Opposite: Gilf Kebir, the mouth of the Abd-el-Malik wadi
Previous double page: the central plateau of Gilf Kebir

A study published by the Geographical Survey of Egypt
established that the **Gilf Kebir** shares many structural similarities with Mars,
as this photograph confirms.

It is a lunar landscape with its dangerously abrupt and vertical slopes.
One could easily lose one's footing or **become disoriented** on its vast, pebble-strewn surface.

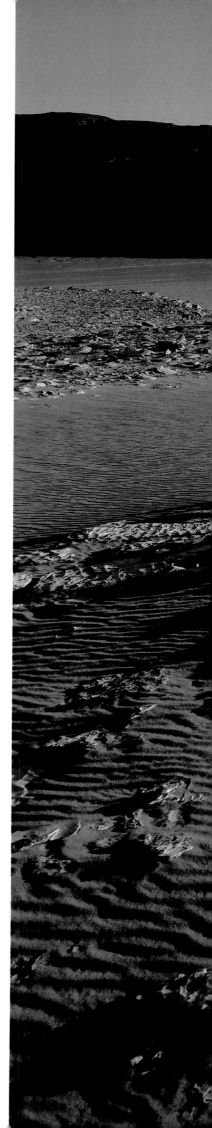

Like most of the wadis in Gilf Kebir,

Abd-el-Malik (opposite) represents a drought-blighted world

where signs of life are no more than a memory.

A handful of withering acacias reminds us that this valley may once have been

the mythical haven of vegetation celebrated by the caravan drivers of eastern Sahara – Zerzura.

The first written account of this oasis appeared in

a 15th-century Arabian text known as 'Hidden Pearls',

which tells of a town 'as white as a pigeon' lying among palm trees, vines and springs.

Here rich lords were to be found as well as a king and queen,

asleep in their castle.

The traveller was warned not to approach the royal couple

but to be satisfied with carrying away their treasure.

Nature followed this advice

and stole the water.

A vast glacis, almost perfectly uniform in shape and hundreds of miles in extent,
stretches to the south of the edge of the Gilf Kebir *cuestra*.
The scattered stones and intermittent inselbergs
suggest compositions of their own natural 'land art'.

The austere, sometimes desolate, landscapes of Gilf Kebir

inspire thoughts that are both highly practical and intensely metaphysical.

Those familiar with the desert will understand this blend of the banal and the lyrical:

day-to-day concern about the level of the petrol gauge

is often accompanied by deep thoughts on a much higher plane.

Embraced between the Mediterranean and the Red Sea,

and traversed by the mighty Nile,

Egypt has a paradoxical relationship with water,

one that wavers between fear and feverish anticipation.

The lakes surrounding Siouah (above) or the tides of the sacred river of the Pharaohs

between Elephantine Island and the east bank,

up near Aswan (opposite),

are vital for supporting life in this inhospitable region.

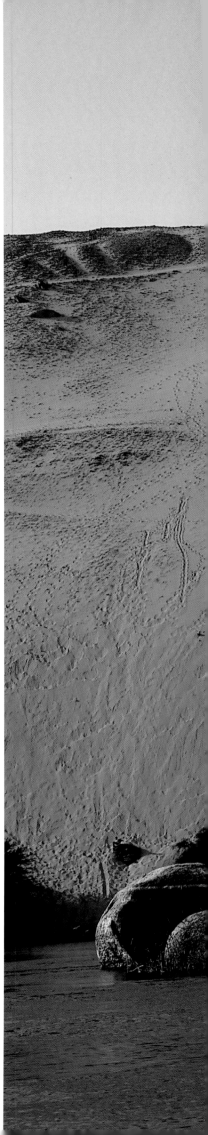

Carved into the flank of a hill on the west bank of the Nile,

the 'sacred river',

the burial places of Pharaonic nobles confirm that the Egyptians reserved this side of the river for the departed.

Nearby stand the ruins of a Coptic church.

Different civilizations have come and gone

but the sacred nature of this region survives.

Arrival in Aswan:

Hamdoulillah (The Lord be praised!)

Our journey took us from the shores of the Atlantic to the banks of the Nile, around 3,000 miles as the crow flies, between Laayoune and Aswan. If you look at a map or globe, you will see that the entire region is designated by the umbrella-term 'Sahara' – its six letters often running the entire length of the Tropic of Cancer. 'Sahara' may be a convenient term but it fails to convey the essence of the region it encompasses. Imagine making a difficult journey, covered in dust, to visit a long-lost friend living in an oasis at the heart of the desert. Upon arrival, his son informs you that his father is 'in the Sahara'. Gradually, the realization dawns that the three huts and four palm trees around you do not constitute the Sahara, the chief characteristic of which Sahara dwellers consider to be solitude. The Greeks had no difficulty in understanding this; they called the barren, uninhabited area **eremos**. The Romans called it **desertus**, whereas the Arabs had a different word to conjure up this often hostile world: Sahrâ. Cartographers subsequently used the latter when filling in the blanks on their maps. This 'common name' stuck and became its official term.

This explains why we prefer to speak of several Saharas instead of a single one. The various parts share some common elements but these are easily outweighed by the differences, and it is these that need to be emphasized rather than glossed over. Each Saharan region is an entity in itself with its own people, tribes, language, traditions and way of life – even the texture of the sand differs between areas.

Each and every one of our experiences was enriching and enlightening, strengthening our attachment to the Sahara and its people. The desert is a never-ending cycle of discovery in itself – a vast, unfathomable, ever changing entity, its vast ergs swept by the untameable, unpredictable wind. Like sailors we would return to port – to Europe – only to prepare for the next departure. Life is lived at its most intense and extreme on those small islands lost in the ocean of the Sahara and at the heart of the regs, where the caravans make their way to the next oasis.

In navigating the Sahara
one becomes a sailor of the sands.

York, June 2001

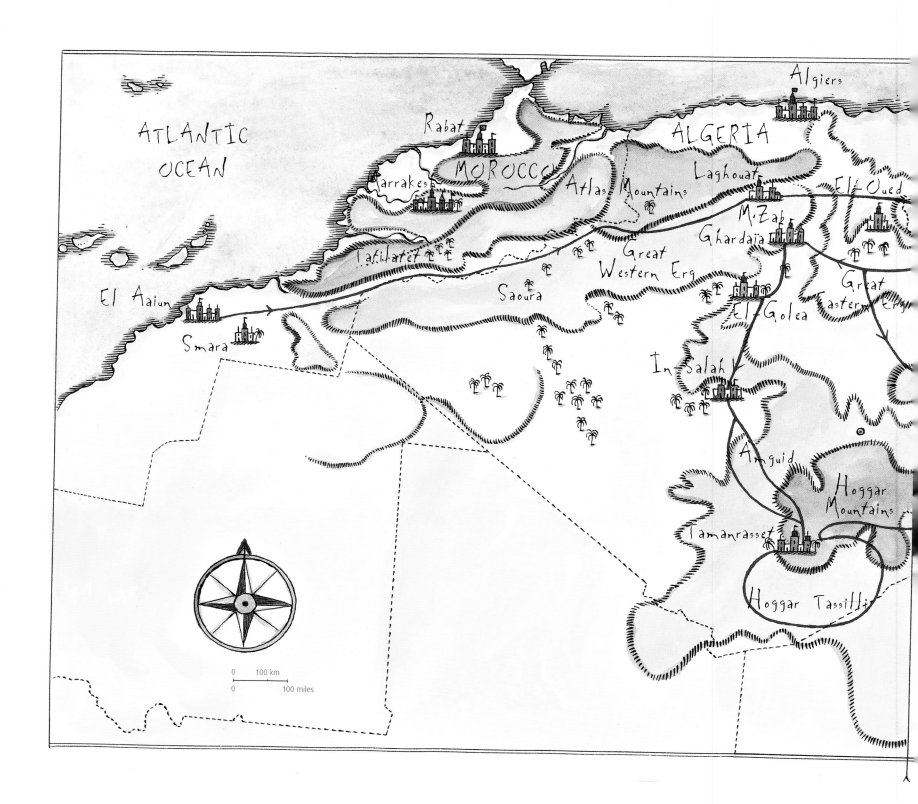

ATLANTIC OCEAN

ALGERIA

Rabat

MOROCCO

Atlas Mountains

Laghouat

Algiers

El Oued

M.Zab

Marrakesh

Ghardaia

Great Western Erg

Great Eastern Erg

Tafilatet

El Aaiun

Saoura

El Golea

Smara

In Salah

Amguid

Hoggar Mountains

Tamanrasset

Hoggar Tassili

0   100 km

0   100 miles

Sahara

the Atlantic to the Nile

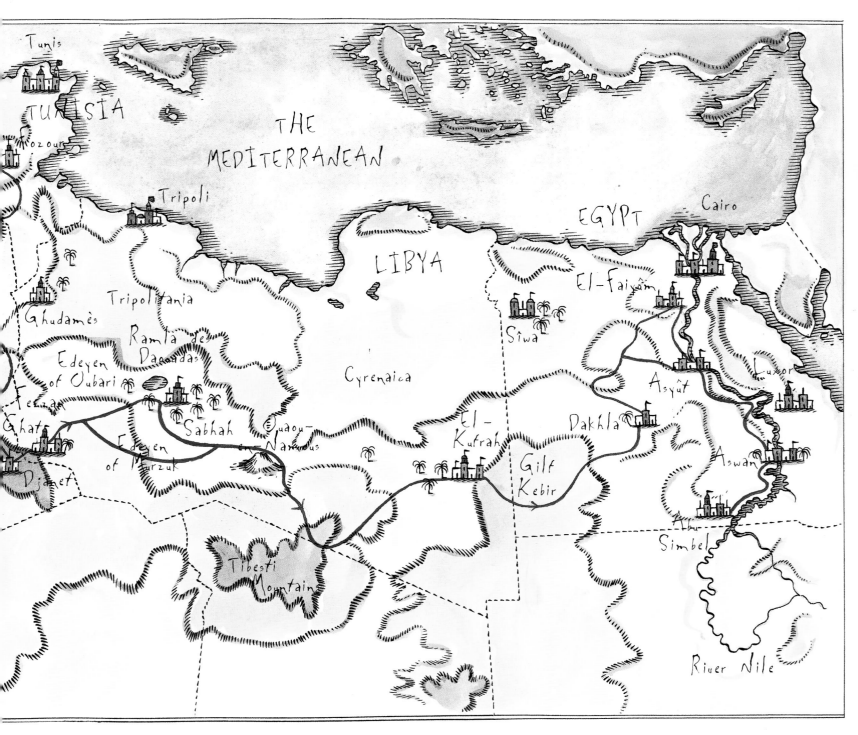

Glossary

Ar = Arabic
Tam = Tamashek (language of the Tuaregs)

Agadir (Ar): fortified barn (in Morocco).

Aguelmam (Tam): natural freshwater reservoir of any size, whether temporary or permanent.

Amenokal (Tam): supreme chief, leader of a group of Tuareg tribes.

Atakor (Tam): the heart of the Hoggar Massif, known as Kuodia in Arabic.

Barkhane (Ar): a crescent-shaped dune with one sheer wind-swept slope and one gentle slope, protected from the wind.

Casbah (Ar): castle or fortress or the area around it; a fortified village.

Cheche (Ar): turban.

Chergui (Ar): warm and dry wind that blows from the southwest (in Morocco).

Chott (Ar): saltwater lake; sebkha.

Dar (Ar): house.

Drinn (Ar): tuft of grass.

Edeyen (Tam): erg with rounded dunes, as opposed to an iguidi, which has pointed dunes.

Enneri (Toubou): dry valley or wadi.

Erg (Ar): sand-sea.

Fech-fech (Ar): powdery sand covered in a thin, hard but brittle crust.

Foggara (Ar): inclined underwater tunnels dug to tap dispersed groundwater in the beds of wadis.

Ghorfa (Ar): unit in a fortified barn (Tunisia).

Ghout (Ar): funnel-shaped palm grove (Algeria).

Guelta (Ar): stretch of natural water fed by a small spring, by rain or by the flooding of the wadi in which it is located.

Guerba (Ar): container made of goat- or sheepskin.

Guezba (Ar): small reeds that surround areas of water (Libya).

Hammada (Ar): rocky, barren plateau, often at or below horizon-level.

Kel (Tam): a prefix meaning 'the people of'.

Ksar (Ar): fortified village.

Markouba (Ar): graminae with a small sandy mound at its base.

Medjbed (Ar): camel track.

Moula-moula (Tam): a sparrow (stonechat) with a black body and a black and white tail, considered to bring luck. The Tuaregs see the moula-moula as a sign of good things to come.

Nebkha (Ar): small sandy hillock, sculpted like an arrow by the wind.

Oued (Ar): wadi – valley or channel of a stream that is dry except in the rainy season.

Ramla (Ar): sand or area of dune (in Libya).

Redjem (Ar): cairn or tumulus – a pile of dry stones (nowadays, a pile of tyres or petrol cans) indicating the route.

Reg (Ar): a barren, firm plain made of compacted gravel and a little sand.

Sebkha (Ar): a barren, enclosed depression with salt deposits.

Seguia (Ar): irrigation channel.

Serir (Berber): flat, hard, barren, stone-covered terrain without vegetation or large rocks.

Sif (Ar): sharp edge of a dune.

Tagelmoust (Tam): indigo-dyed fabric from Nigeria, sewn into narrow bands and wound round the head to hide the forehead and mouth.

Tamashek (Tam): language of the Tuaregs.

Tamedjida (Ar): open-air mosque.

Tamenast (Tam): a metal plate – beaten copper on the outside, smooth interior.

Tassili (Tam): sandstone plateau, often eroded and criss-crossed by a network of valleys.

Tifinar (Tam): Berber script (made up only of vowels).

Zaouïa (Ar): religious groups or setting.

Zeriba (Ar): reed hut.

Index
of place names

All photographs by **Alain Sèbe**,
except those on the following pages:
8, 17, 26 (centre right), 34-35, 39, 40,
42 (top right, bottom right), 143, 144, 147,
148, 149, 163, 176-177, 179, 182 and 184,
which were by **Berny Sèbe**.

Editor
Nathalie Bailleux

Art editor
Nancy Dorking

Design and layout
François Chevret

© Hachette Livre 2001
This edition published by
Hachette Illustrated UK, Octopus Publishing Group,
2-4 Heron Quays, London E14 4JP

English translation produced by JMS Books LLP
Translation © Octopus Publishing Group

A CIP catalogue for this book is available from the British
Library

ISBN: 1 84430 026 9

Printed by Tien Wah, Singapore